Table Of Content

01	CHOOSING YOUR DOMAIN NAME
06	CHOOSING YOUR HOSTING & WEBSITE
11	INSTALLING A WEBSITE
17	FIND THE SEARCH TERMS FOR YOUR BUSINESS
22	WHY OPTIMISE YOUR WEBSITE?
28	TOOLS TO CHECK YOUR SITE
31	SOME OF MY FAVORITE TOOLS/SOFTWARE/SERVICES

CHOOSING YOUR DOMAIN NAME

THE FIRST STEP TO YOUR NEW WEBSITE

Firstly, what is a domain name?

It's the unique identifier given to your website by the Domain Name System (DNS).

If you want to have a website, you need a domain name.

The most difficult part about owning a domain name is choosing it!

The amount of times I get asked 'What is the perfect domain name for a business?' and have to say, it depends on the business type.

That always seems like a bit of a lame answer, but I have to say that it is the right one!

As more and more websites get loaded onto the internet and search engines get more demanding, many people say you should have a keyword in your domain name.

Now whilst I think this is a good idea if you are only selling one product or service, this usually isn't the case for most businesses.

They also often say put your locality into the domain name but what happens when you want to expand. I believe locality is best placed in good SEO strategies. We'll get to those in future units.

When you look at the top brands, being called Apple or Pepsi never did any harm to those businesses, so going with your catchy business name and brand, will work if you build it effectively.

One last thought, I use .com extensions and the reason for this is, in my opinion, people prefer .com to anything else. I use any other type of extension as sites that link to my main site. These sit quietly doing things like hosting a training platform or specific landing pages.

I do think that if you are based in the UK or even selling to the UK market, having both the .com and .co.uk domains will work well. Just divert your .co.uk domain to your .com domain.

So, the steps you need to take are:

Tasks

1. **Decide on a name for your website and for use on all of your branding.**

2. **Head over to a domain reseller, I prefer: Namecheap but there are plenty out there that you can use.**

3. **Type in your chosen name and see if your domain is available.**

4. **Register an account with them**

5. **Take note of your account details especially your password**

6. **Purchase your domain(s) and SSL certificate**

Step 1:

Decide on a name for your website and for use on all of your branding.

Your name will be your brand, choose carefully.

Take a close look at what the customer will see when they find your name. Does it look good when you write it down on a piece of paper?

Try not to add hyphens as they are not easy to type. However sometimes a hyphen can make the domain name look better. So use with care.

Step 2:

Head over to a domain reseller, I prefer: Namecheap but there are plenty out there that you can use.

Purchasing a domain name is relatively easy.

They are usually bought for a year at a time but you can buy for longer if you wish.

Some people have said that Google may rank you quicker if you buy for longer periods of time, but I haven't seen evidence of that.

One thing you do need to do, is to make sure that your domain is signed up for automatic renewal. This ensures that you never lose your domain.

Never let anyone transfer your domain at any time, if you lose this, it will be hard to get back. There is usually a facility to lock down transfers. I recommend you do this.

Step 3:

Type in your chosen name and see if your domain is available.

This is the part where you have spent time deciding on a name and then you type it into the search engine and find that someone has beaten you to it.

As a rule of thumb, if the .com has been bought, leave well alone. Have another think and see if you can find another suitable name.

If you really want the domain, you usually have an option to contact the owner to see if they would be happy to sell, however it will usually cost you a lot more to do that.

Get yourself the .com as your main domain name and possibly buy the .net, or local country extension.

A tip as well, is to type your chosen domain into Google search to see what comes up, you don't want to find yourself in an argument with another business that trades very similar to your business.

Step 4:

Register an account with them

You will not be able to buy from any hosting company unless you register with them. They need to have your details on file as a legal requirement.

Buying domains in most countries can be straight forward but there are a few countries who ask for passport details/proof of ownership before you can purchase a domain.

Step 5:

Take note of your account details especially your password

It really amazes me how people do not take note of their passwords and account details. I recommend that if you are working online, you need a small password note book or any form of password storage that works for you.

Most people forget what they've done after a few weeks and then cannot remember the hosting company or password. You need this information to get access to your account when you are ready to go live with your website.

Step 6

Purchase your domain(s) and SSL certificate

When you purchase your domain, I strongly recommend that you also buy an SSL certificate. This will tell the world and Google that your site is safe to use. If you choose not to add this certificate to your site, you will more than likely find than any visitors to your site will get a warning that the site is not safe. Not a good start to a new business!

This is happening more now that Google has said that it wants to clean up the sites that they show.

An SSL Certificate shows that you have proved you own the site and there are records being held to that effect. It is not a difficult process and it gives you more credibility for your website.

If you have your own hosting account, you can often use one SSL certificate for several sites, making it a lot more cost effective.

Again, I really like Namecheap for SSL certificates as they do not overcharge and are simple to set up.

I think this about wraps up my information on domain names.

I hope you now feel that you know enough to go and buy your domain.

CHOOSING YOUR HOSTING & WEBSITE

Firstly, What is Web Hosting?

Web hosting is a service that allows individuals and businesses to make their website accessible via the Internet.

To do this you need to buy a domain and then pay for it to be hosted for you.

If you want to have a website, you need a domain name and hosting.

In the last e-book we talked about a domain name.

Now we look at how to use the domain name with the hosting to build the platform for our website.

Hosting is a cloudbased platform we need in order to showcase our website. It is the place that enables the world to see our products and services. It is the platform that enables us to be open 24/7.

Many people buy a domain and get a shock when they are told that they need hosting as well! So often they go for the first hosting company they see because they panic.

You can get hosting cheap, but you only get what you pay for and so you need to answer a few questions before you sign up to any hosting.

* Will my site be hosted in the right location for my business needs?

* How long am I tied into the hosting plan?

* If I get a lot of visitors at any one time, will the host plan be able to accommodate it?

* What is the downtime rate? (You want 99% plus, ideally.)

* Will I have access to a help desk quickly if I

So, the steps you need to take are:

Tasks

1. Decide on the appropriate location for your hosting.

2. Do a Google Search for a Hosting Supplier, I prefer: Namecheap but there are plenty out there that you can use.

3. Explore the Hosting Plans and choose one.

4. Register an account with them. Remember to take note of your account details especially your password.

5. Purchase your hosting plan.

6. Wait for the instructions to arrive via email

Step 1:

Decide on the appropriate location for your hosting.

As a rule, you usually ensure that your hosting is based in the country you are targeting.

If you are a UK based business, you are better to ensure the server that hosts your website is based in the UK.

Obviously, if you are an online business with no fixed premises or a blogger, these guidelines are less important.

Step 2:

Do a Google Search for a Hosting Supplier

I prefer: Namecheap but there are plenty out there that you can use.

When you scour the different hosting plans, you will find the starting range can be as low as a few dollars a month to hundreds a month.

Step 3:

Explore the Hosting Plans and choose one.

When you scour the different hosting plans, you will find the starting range can be as low as a few dollars a month to hundreds a month.

My advice to you, is to decide if this will be your only site or if you will have multiple sites and also how many visitors you hope to attract to your site.

For one small site, with a few visitors a day, the cheapest plan can often be ok.

If you expect to be attracting many visitors to your site, then a better plan would be a wiser investment.

Start with a plan of about £15 per month and upgrade if you need to.

Upgrades are instant so there is no need to pay for bandwidth and speed that you won't need.

Want More Tips and Advice?

Visit Me at: www.sueberry.com

Step 4:

Register an account with them. Remember to take note of your account details especially your password.

Of course, the hosting company are there to help you choose the best plan for your circumstances, so don't be afraid to ask questions.

I like to use the chat box that they make available. In most cases you will get an answerr almost immediately from them.

Hosting companies tend to have online support 24 hours a day. If they don't, they will answer your questions as soon as they possibly can.

Step 5:

Purchase your hosting plan.

You will not be able to buy from any hosting company unless you register with them. They need to have your details on file as a legal requirement.

Buying hosting packages in most countries can be straight forward but there are a few countries who ask for passport details/proof of ownership before you can purchase.

Step 6:

Wait for the instructions to arrive via email

It will take a short while for the hosting company to set up your new account.

They will contact you by email as soon as they have completed the process.

In the emails that you receive, there will be several lots of instructions and important information. I suggest that you print these off and also save to a folder on your desktop for easy retreival.

Series

HOSTING TIPS

What to Think About

- ✔ Set a budget as it's easy to keep adding on extras that you may never need
- ✔ Decide if you want to use the hosting package of your domain provider or not.
- ✔ Buy hosting to suit your needs. Often a small package will do fine initially
- ✔ Decide if you want to add multiple sites to that hosting, if you do then maybe a reseller account would work better for you.

INSTALLING A WEBSITE

Now the exciting time is here, you are going to build and upload a website to your hosting plan.

You've a couple of choice here:

1. Get it designed for you
2. Build it yourself!

Now only you know whether you are able to build your own website.

Many hosting companies offer ready made templates where you just insert images and text. These can be perfect when you are just starting out.

I love WordPress and so that is my preferred website type.

It's so flexible and has many themes and plugins available for free. It means that every site I build can be structured to the needs of my client and their business.

There are many training videos available to help you learn to build a website/blog.

If you choose to get your site built for you, there are five things that you really should be aware of.

After carrying out some random reviews of websites owned by businesses, it was all too clear that many were failing to deliver on the basic requirements needed for a successful business site.

What was more alarming was that these websites were often built by 'expert' developers, supposedly working in the best interests of their clients.

There are many reasons why this would happen, and perhaps not something that should be covered in this article. So instead, let's take a quick look at some of the most common mistakes, and how to quickly move towards resolving them.

6 Important Considerations

- ✔ SSL Security
- ✔ Search Engine Ranking
- ✔ Mobile Optimisation
- ✔ Page Speed
- ✔ Image Optimisation
- ✔ Web Schema

SSL Security

From January 2017 Google Chrome started marking sites without SSL certificate as unsecure.

Google Chrome alerts your visitor that you have an unsecure site if it cannot find the SSL Certificate!

Now this has taken a little while to roll out but it is picking up momentum really quickly now and when it reaches your site, if you've not installed the SSL Certificate just what are the consequences to your business?

HTTP is seen as an unsecure protocol. HTTPS is seen as secure.

An SSL Certificate - (HTTPS) Offers Three Layers of Protection:

1. It encrypts your data
2. It stops data being modified
3. It proves you are who you say you are, stopping 'middlemen/phishing'

Google are starting to rank sites with HTTPS higher than those that have just HTTP. So you might never see a first page ranking in the future unless you have that little added protection of an SSL Cetificate and those little letters - HTTPS.

Search Engine Ranking

The primary objective of any business website should be to attract new customers to that business, unless of course the intention is to deliver supporting information after a sale has been made.

Assuming that a business wants to attract new customers, it should also be okay to assume that ranking in Google or Bing might be helpful.

There are certain expectations that a search engine applies, and to be truthful, these are pretty obvious, although far to often overlooked.

Local businesses should clearly display their name, address and phone number (NAP) on each page, and most especially the home page. A map is also helpful but perhaps not as imperative.

It is also important to display links to an About Us, a Contact Us, A Terms of Use and a Privacy Policy from each page.

In addition, Google expects to see at least one page that connects all other pages on the site. This is most effectively served up as a site map, but make sure this is also linked to from the home page.

That pretty much covers the fundamentals, without getting too geeky. Of course, it never hurts to put a video up there on the home page as well as some images too, as long as they are correctly tagged or labeled.

Mobile Optimisation

It is undoubted that most searches now take place on mobile phones.

Google fully understand that, as it was probably them who told us about it in the first place.

Accordingly, Google have just announced they are giving preferential ranking to sites that are fully mobile compliant.

This doesn't mean seeing what a site looks like on a mobile. It is a bit more in-depth than that.

Again there is no need to delve too deep here as Google kindly offer a page for testing the compliance of a site. That link can be found in the resources section at the end of this article.

The plain truth here is, ignore this advice and the days of ranking are numbered.

Page Speed

This has a bit to do with mobile but is also embedded in the history of web development.

As websites and computers became ever faster, there was a thirst for more visually stunning sites.

The problem here was that as sites became ever more visual, they also became increasingly slower to load. It is a very clearly stated fact that a site which takes more than 3 seconds to load will start to lose visitors.

People do not have the patience to wait in these times of instant gratification. If a page takes 5 seconds to load, then at least 25% of visitors would have turned away.

By the time the load speed has reached double digits, the only person to remain might be the site owner and the web designer, pretty much everyone else will have gone already.

This very clearly goes against the purpose of the website and so is one more critical factor that needs to be understood and addressed.

Again, Google help out here with a very handy tool, which again can be found at the foot of this article.

The results of running these tests are given with explanation but these are not really for the non-technical site owner.

There are some things that can be done quite easily to speed up a website, and some others that would baffle the boffins.

Image Optimisation

An important aspect that affects most of the above is about how images are delivered to site visitors.

There is a tendency to put any image up on a site and not bother about optimising it.

However, if that image is of a higher resolution than is necessary, or if the original image is of a different size to what is ultimately displayed, the page will take longer to load, and will in turn risk a loss of visitors.

There are various ways to optimise images, but there is an easy way that is ready to implement.

Go back to the Google Page Speed Tool and scroll right down to the bottom of the results page.

Hidden away where most people don't go is a nice downloadable zip of any offending images, already resized as Google wants to see them

Just replace the images in that file with the images on the website and that is the job effectively done.

Web Schema

This topic is maybe moving into the realms of geeky but it has to be discussed nonetheless.

If a website is a book and the web pages are chapters, then Schema are the author notes on the back page.

Schema basically tells the search engines everything they need to know about a site, its content and in the case of local businesses, the products, services and location.

As the focus shifts ever more towards mobile optimised pages, schema becomes ever more critical.

The reason for this is that schema tells the search engines what they need to know to serve a web page to a mobile browser, and then the page delivers enough information to deliver the call to action for the end user.

In a sense, it is the ultimate information partnership, and clear to see why the search engines all work together in their acceptance of schema.

A site can be tested for schema either using the webmaster tools of each search engine or by using the tools provided on schema.org.

That about sums up a quite simplistic overview of some critical elements that should be understood about ranking a local business website.

Series

FIND THE SEARCH TERMS FOR YOUR BUSINESS

Assemble a list of search words (aka keywords) that your target audience will use to find your products and services.

When your target market is searching Google or other search engines for the product or service you have on offer, you need to be able to get in front of them every time.

Start by asking a few of your customers what they search for or would search for if they needed to find your business.

Write down a list of phrases you think they would search for.

It is a good exercise as often we have not really given a thought to how people find us on the internet.

Keyword Research

Your keyword list is the start to finding what people are searching for to find the products or services that you sell.

Single keywords can be competitive, so I would suggest that you look at a phrase rather than a keyword.

You almost certainly don't need to get yourself on the first page of Google for a single keyword because it is usually too generic.

For example, if you are a wedding planner in Spain but your target market only lives in the UK, a keyword of 'wedding' would bring a lot of people to your site but a huge percentage of those people would not be in the right country, they most likely wouldn't be considering a wedding abroad and they are generally just doing research.

Now if we add 'wedding planner' this will tighten the search and bring you more targeted views, but they still will not be a perfect target audience.

So, if we looked at 'wedding planner in Spain' or 'overseas wedding planner' we would be targeting those couples that are considering getting married abroad.

A much better choice of keyword to use on our website and if we are going to be spending money advertising, I'm sure you'll not want to throw your money away on non-buyers!

Let's look at another business:

A plumber.

A plumber wants to attract customers in his local area, but the word 'plumber' could mean different things to different people, also many people research that keyword to learn about work opportunities too.

If you think about the needs of your client. They have a boiler that has stopped working, it's winter and they need the fix as quickly as they can.

What will they type into the search engines?

Possibly 'emergency boiler repair' or 'qualified boiler engineer near me'

When they have a problem, they will type more words to get the right result faster!

So how could you improve on the keyphrases above?

I would add locality and an urgency keywords in the key phrase. Now Google are getting good at local searches however, I think when your site is new, all little tweaks add up to faster success.

Here's what we now have:

'Emergency boiler repair specialist Grimsby' and 'qualified emergency boiler engineer Grimsby'

Did you see what I have done?

The second phrase did not have emergency in it. If you want people to know you are there for them in an emergency, let them know. It won't stop your site being show for non-emergency work.

Let's look at a Garden Centre

What would their customers be looking for?

Local, opening times, seasonal plants, café, advice, maybe a home delivery.

So, the keywords/keyphrases need to include some of the above words.

I would look at 'local garden centre with café, Southampton' – for people wanting to make a trip out and buy a few plant and have food or coffee too.

Obviously you would change the town if you weren't in Southampton!

Maybe 'garden centre, home delivery Southampton area.'

Or 'Garden centre with seasonal plants Southampton' maybe change the 'seasonal' to 'bedding'

For those that need opening times, 'Southampton garden centre open everyday'

I hope you are starting to understand what I am doing here.

I am using my key phrases to copy what my potential customers could be searching for.

There are many tools that you can use for the keyword/phrase research.

Google has it's own keyword tool but you need to set up an account so I suggest that to start, you simply drop your keyword/phrase into Google search and see how many searches you get and try a chrome extension called Keywords Everywhere. It's simple to use but does only work on Google Chrome.

It has some good instructions on how to set it up too.

Here's a couple of screen shots I got when I typed in 'plumbers in grimsby'

The information this plugin gives you is good to see how your potential customers are searching

I dropped 'garden centre, home delivery, Southampton area' into Google and what I got was 16,600,000 searched. Now that is not accurate for Southampton UK, these searches probably include a Southampton in other parts of the world so I'm going to add UK and see the difference.

If you are based in Southampton you would get more accurate searches.

Currently I am in the Canary Islands so that alters my results slightly.

What it does show you is that people are searching these terms. One interesting thing that I observed when looking at the results, was that I found it hard to find a real garden centre to visit that I could go and hand choose my plants and then get them delivered to my home for me.

Two things here:

1. Most of the Google finds were for online buying and delivery. Not quite Google's target market so if you use this keyword/phrase as a real garden centre that offers delivery, you could quite easily start to rank high on Google.

2. This could be the case around the country. So maybe an opportunity all of you Garden Centres!

Tip: The value under the competition column shows you how difficult that keyword might be to get ranked. 1 is harder than 0.36 for example. This isn't an exact science and so only use as a guideline.

Tip: To get faster rankings, higher sales conversions, and many more pages indexed in Google - work on finding the best long-tail keywords for your audience!

Series

Now you have some Keywords...

Now you have some keywords, I want you to think about your website. Ideally each page should have at least one of these keywords inserted into your text and also add a couple of related keywords.

If you do this, Google will really understand that you have a website that is of useful value to your potential customers.

If you have a large website, it can be a bit tedious implementing this strategy but most of you will only have a small site and so making this a 'good practice' task for every page you build will be really valuable to you as time goes on.

So to recap:

1. Use your main keyword one to three times on your page

2. Use two to three related keywords once on your page.

WHY OPTIMISE YOUR WEBSITE?

Moving on to the next subject to consider: Optimising your website. Why should you bother?

There's a simple answer to this question.

The search engines want to perfect the results that they find for their customers. They want their experience to be as perfect as possible.

So as time moves forward Google and the other search engines, improve the way they search for and find the correct results for people.

You need to help them along the way and develop a win-win relationship.

Google has recently made a lot of changes to it's expectations of websites. It will first show sites that offer the information it needs, then it will show the nearest to that.

If you choose to ignore Google, chances are your site will only get found if someone types your domain into the search bar.

But 98% of these searchers don't even know you exist so they won't know the name of your website!

I think we all realise that doing anything online can be a drain on the cash. That doesn't mean it's not a vital exercise for any business. Google make some statements and SEO businesses jump on it and try to get you to part with cash.

I actually have a few tricks for Website Optimizing that comes free or very low cost..

The main areas that we need to make sure are in order on our website are that they are:

1. Mobile Friendly

2. Fast Loading

3. User Friendly

4. Visitor Focused

5. Clean Looking and Easy to Read

There could be more, but these are what I will focus on here. These five are enough to be getting on with and they will make the most dramatic changes to your search engine rankings.

Mobile Friendly

I guess by now you understand the frustrations of doing an online search on your phone, only to find the screen can't hold all of the information or it's just not easy to read. Maybe some some elements are missing or maybe you try to do something but it just doesn't work well.

So frustrating!

This is exactly why Google and other search engines want businesses to offer a mobile friendly site for their viewers.

It is one of the most important measures they make.

So it makes sense to get it right.

In the past the websites that were build were of a fixed size, then flexible sizing was introduced.

Most people having a new site developed will have it made in a mobile and tablet friendly way, but maybe not if you use someone that hasn't moved with the times!

There's not many of these web builders around but there's one or two and I've met some of them. They just won't or can't keep up with the times!

Just be aware, sometimes doing a site on the cheap could bring you more problems than you would need.

Sometimes you will be told that you need a mobile site as well as traditional site. Again in the past that was often true but nowadays any good designer will be able to build a mobile friendly site that works on all the relevant platforms - desktops,tablets and mobiles.

Tip: Keep page titles concise nd relevant to your viewers seach terms.

Fast Loading

A pet hate of mine is a slow loading website. Websites should really load in under 2 seconds.

When I am searching for a site, I want to see it really quickly and the truth is, we all do.

We leave to move on to the next result if loading takes too long. That's lost customers!

Get fast loading pages. If you have slow loading pages you must work on decreasing this time.

Google also want you to have fast loading websites. They penalise slow loading sites by not showing them, unless they have no other similar site to show. So if you have competition, if their site loads quicker than yours, watch out as they might just be getting your potential clients and you never realised!

So how do you know how quickly your site loads?

Here is one of the free tools that you can use to test the load time of your site on both mobiles and desktops.

https://developers.google.com/speed/pagespeed/

This page will show us how fast the page loads and also what you need to do to address the issues.

Make sure to check both mobile and desktop speeds. Be aware that the mobile results are the important ones.

On this page you will see tabs for Mobile Speed and Desktop Speed.

Always check both.

The nearest you can get to 100% the better.

It's also good because Google tells you what you should put right to make your site more appealing and useable for them.

User Friendly

Okay, so what do I mean by user-friendly? Well, I mean it should do exactly what you say it will. No broken links or iimages that can't load. No forms that you can't fill in.

Payment pages should work well and be simple to navigate and understand.

What could be more frustrating to your potential customer, than to type in all of their details, eagerly wanting to buy a product and the link to the payment site won't work!

My guess is you will probably lose them at this point. THey won't keep trying, there's other pressing needs that need to be sorting in everyone's lives.

Will they come back? Doubtful!

What you need to do, is to systematically check every page of your website for missing images and broken links.

It's mundane but do it once and then you can almost forget it.

Perhaps it's best to check it every few months.

If your website is on the WordPress platform, you could add a plugin to alert you of any broken links on your pages. I find this invaluable as it's a real time saver.

I will list a few other great plugins at the end of this book.

Visitor Focused

I keep banging on about businesses getting their heads around being 'Customer Focused'.

I actually find it hard to get some people to make the change from having a website that is selling how clever or important they or their businesses are, to understanding exactly what their potential buyers want to see.

There is so much information available to people, that your website needs to stand out above the rest.

Google wants you to offer exactly what these people want to read. You need your site to be the one do this. Not your competitors.

Using search terms and them expanding is by far the best method.

The about is page is where you write 'about you and your business'.

The Landing pages (expecially the home page) are for answering the need of the reader, making them feel they must learn more about your product or service because you have exactly what they are looking for. It should draw them in without the big sell.

There's a lot around that explains the concept of story telling so I'll just point you in the direction of one great free course (3 videos).

http://www.5minutemarketingmakeover.com

You get:

* Why your customers aren't buying

* 5 ways to sharpen your message

* A look at a website that works

They offer some great training but that's up to you whether you need them to teach you more after you've watch the 3 free videos.

Give the reader an experience that makes them trust you. Most people don't do this, they just sell or talk about themselves.

Remember people want solutions first, next comes the trust!

Clean Looking and Easy to Read

Although I don't want to focus on this statement too much, the powers that be, state most people read as though they were about 7 years old as they are browsing the internet. Not sure that I agree but they must be able to substantiate it. What I do know, is that people scan and move on.

So with that being said, the best definitely a lot of white space, relevant images, easy to understand text and an instruction of what to do next really does improve sales.

Keep it clean, simple and explain what the reader needs to do next!

When you're planning your new site, or looking at your new one, always ask others how they enjoyed the experience of reading through it and/or what they would expect to see.

Then you put your buyers head on and test it out.

You've only a few seconds to make someone read on. Get it right first time!

White space is good. It stops a site looking too busy.

Your headlines need to be captivating. If you don't draw a reader in by your headline, you may lose them completely.

Produce well written content that is clear and concise. As I've stated earlier a big consideration is that people like to scan, so bullet points can often work well near the top of the page. They scan your well written bullet points and then move down the page for more detail.

Determining your business goals and building a storyboard at the start of your website build should ensure you have a real guide to get your website user friendly and well performing.

TOOLS TO CHECK YOUR SITE

There are two tools that I use, one is a Google Chrome extension and the other is a WordPress plugin.

Both do slightly different things.

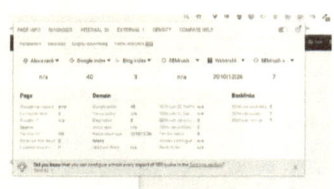

SEOQuake is a free tool that you install onto your Google Chrome search bar. It allows you to see issues with any website. It also shows you how to fix them.

There is a premium package but I think the free version is plenty good enough when you're starting out.

Go to the 3 dots on the right hand side of your tool bar.

Click onn more tools, then on extensions. Search for SEO Quake and install. If it won't install, turn the developer mode on. Download and turn it off again.

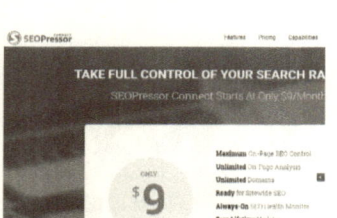

SEOPressor

This is a premium plugin for wordPress but is one of the best in my opinion for such a small cost.

SEO is becoming so complicated now that it's no longer possible to do it without an expert's help.
Even if you know your SEO, it would still take up too much of your time and keep you away from doing what you really want to do.

SEOPressor Connect makes SEO so easy and quick that anybody could do it.

https://sueberry.com/seo

FINAL WORD

I hope that I have packed enough information into this ebook to help you get started.

I am sure that in most cases, a good website developer will know all of the information that I have talked about.

I just believe that as a business owner, you can't have too much information. Especially when it comes to your website as it is your shop window 24/7!

My advice to you is to try to stay up to date with Google's criteria, as it is always being updated.

You need to be in the know. If it's not your thing, get a professional to do it for you and feed back. But stay aware!

Use any new product/service you launch as an opportunity to review your website.

Is your message still current, could your message be tweaked to grab the attention of viewers?

Check what your competitors are doing, don't get left behind.

What ever you do, don't forget to diarise a time every few months to revisit your site.

It can't work well for you without your input!

Then be proud of yourself as you are doing far more than most business owners!

LIST OF RELATED BOOKS

Before you buy a domain name, take a look at some of my advice about choosing the right domain name for your business needs.

More Info here

In this booklet, I try to run through the things that you need to be aware of, before you buy hosting or commission a web build.

More Info here

Keyword research is a bit of an art, so, in this booklet, I outline a simple strategy to get you started.

More Info here

SOME OF MY FAVORITE TOOLS/SOFTWARE/SERVICES

I only add the products or services that I use.

 A reliable and competitively priced company providing domains & hosting

 Cost Effective Hosting for beginners with a great Customer Care Service

 A choice of SSL certificates to suit your website needs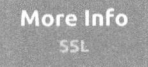

 A plugin for WordPress sitest o alert you when links get broken on your site.

 You can redirect errors to any existing page or custom link (globally).

 Takes care of your WordPress SEO, well worth a look.

RESOURCES:

Google Mobile-Friendly Test:
 https://www.google.co.uk/webmasters/tools/mobile-friendly/

Google Page Speed Tools:
https://developers.google.com/speed/pagespeed/

Google Structured Data Testing Tool:
https://search.google.com/structured-data/testing-tool/

Storybrand
http://www.5minutemarketingmakeover.com/

THANK YOU

I Welcome Your Feedback

feel free to get in touch with me for any feedback or questions

www.sueberry.com/contact-us

www.ingramcontent.com/pod-product-compliance
Lightning Source LLC
Chambersburg PA
CBHW030550220526
45463CB00007B/3046